BITCHES' BREW

Cover Art & Chapter Art by D. Pratt

Black Minds Publishing is a national publications platform centered around the personal and professional growth of artists and creatives of the Black diaspora. At Black Minds Publishing we aim to give more visibility to raw artistic works, both literary and visual, that center on the healing process of the Black mind, body and spirit. We aren't concerned with the rigid expectations of academia or the "supposed to's" of artistic gatekeepers and instead choose to prioritize genuine works that have meaningful impact for its readers.

Names: Safiya Washington

Title: Bitches' Brew

Description: Philadelphia, PA: Black Minds Publishing [2022]

Identifiers: 978-1-7375490-0-0

BLACK MINDS
PUBLISHING

THIS ONE'S FOR ALL MY PEOPLE IN THE STRUGGLE

AARUN SIMON
DAVID PRATT
RIENNE SCOTT
NINA LYRISPECT BALL
KIRWYN SUTHERLAND
ANGELIQUE PALMER
ROSCOE BURNEMS
JOHN S BLAKE
JERICHO BROWN
RANDALL HORTON
TARA BETTS
SHANEKA BRIGGS
MARIE FRANCOIS LEWIS
TYRA AKANKE CHERISE WASHINGTON
REMICA L. BINGHAM-RISHER
TYEHIMBA JESS
MARIAHDESSA TALLIE
ASHLEE HAZE
BRITTANY ROGERS
MORGAN PARKER
DAMARIS HILL
DUSTIN PEARSON
JEANANN VERLEE
KITA MARSHALL
GISELE BUCHANAN
NABILA LOVELACE
PATRICK ROSAL
GREGORY PARDLO
SHAKEEMA SMALLS
YABA BLAY
TAUREAN CUTTEN
SINNEA DOUGLAS
KUSH THOMPSON
JESICA BLANDON
CAMONGHNE FELIX

Table of Contents

WHEN
I
WAS
YOUNG
I
RECALL,
SOME
PHILLIP
HALL
SHIT.

I   Want to Be

An Erasure of Gavin DeGraw's I Don't Want To Be

I don't need   an   other
      guard.
  don't need   an   other
    specialist.
I don't have to be an   other,
      two   in one,
part   going   knowing
    coming from.

I don't want to be
    what I've been   lately.

I'm tired   looking 'round rooms wondering
  who I'm supposed to be.
I don't want to be anything other.

I'm surrounded   everywhere I turn
I'm surrounded   everywhere I turn
I'm   everywhere I turn
am I the only one   ?
I can't be the only one

I don't want to be

All I have   is   me and
I'm tired of   wondering what I gotta do
    to be
      me

We are the Ones Born into the Belly of the Beast

In New York, my mother fought a rat
on a subway platform for an ice cream sandwich.
On the drive home from center city she exclaims
I swear I got mugged by a rat before!
Some fights are worth conceding.
She'd never been so afraid.
As he stood up on his hind legs,
& let out a low sharp hiss.
she gave up her cone and ran.
Some fights aren't worth flesh.

My friends & I spent my last Brooklyn summer in knuckles
& knotted guts.
Mommy says that's the thing about us New Yorkers,
we bred to dodge hissing dumpsters by the bus stop.
Our homes are always burning or being sold.
Even the rats are always ready to fight to live;
Cause Brooklyn hard on anybody.
& our bodies learned to protect
& save the mischief we could manage.

& If you ask me
you don't know a city until you've met its beasts;
Until you've fist forced yourself into the landscape
& the rats don't even try you.

Cheeks For Face

Aged 8, had
big ol' naps
two fat afro puffs
two missing front teeth,
& two bare brown legs quivering cold in bathroom stall
because of cackling Sasha, one stall over, who tossed my jeans
a denim lump soaking in a toilet bowl.
that lead to one naked lunch room dash to shame,
that playground.

All concrete and metal.
all wind carrying small figure.
all the voices taunting Khalif saying
"she rag doll small."
one boy.
one crowd,
watching how fast he sweeps me up
tosses me over his shoulder
bragging about my light and we spin,
and I fall
pavement to face. I know how impact feels
when no one catches you. but that playground
likes to spread its black asphalt
gives gifts before picture day, the biggest bruise under my left eye.

Those eyes thought they knew what they were doing.
trying to fleek our arches from natural to grown.
one eye closed
tongue to lips
trying to level
play America's Next Top Model
with Frankenstein's hands.
holding eyebrow shapers like crayons - they ain't.

4

Sarah, whose eyebrow we had to draw back on,
learned first - it wasn't on purpose.

We didn't know growing up meant making boxing rings of playgrounds.
that could thin the face to something less round.
or meant always having a story to tell.
who knew there was another way to live
who knew there was another way to learn
there was no one to tell us that we didn't have to spread
into people so completely different than who we were.

True Blue & Tight Like Glue

A Golden Shovel

We were triplet fairies, for the length of a song. We
danced, held Diana up with a single palm, for real,
our bare feet flirted with the wood. We ran to cool,

Vanessa stretched out in front of the cows fence. We
turned our faces into the grass & inhaled, Amanda left.
This how us urban girls make home of farm school,

strip the water for every native species. We
non-natives made South Hall a place to lurk
we tagged everything a hood, ours, even late,

in the crowd around Diana's first lap dance. We
mayhem in drag, invoking every laugh to strike.
Gully be our shirt's cut for powder puff, straight

stroll out in bandanas and war paint. We
weekend train rides home when we sing
of families blended by boroughs and sin.

Stuffed in bleachers, burrito wrapped, we
in blankets that are always way too thin,
refereeing fights caused from all the gin.

Gathering gossip in Sunday morning recap rants, we
a Saturday of scraping every edge feeling for Jazz,
the liquor soaked pineapples cooling summer's June.

In everything that ain't supposed to be ours, we
are bodies posed loud for selfies trying not to die
& we laugh at this town, we won't know soon.

To Come From

A Prose Poem

To come from: a relative definition, not to be confused with home. [Meaning] the first street corner to share kiss of lips & concrete. The first boy to creep something extra into his smile. You can almost taste the first strawberry on her lips. To come from is to belong to what's already gone. The fleeting. Temporary. For days home feels like a word you can only say alone. When the corner stained with your knee's flesh don't know you. Long after the streets that have watched you grow have white washed their brownstones, altered love's wingspan to carry different time zones. To come from is soul. Blues. Funk. The base when you wind your hips round the darkest roots and still belong everywhere or nowhere. Someone will ask where you've acquired such a twisted tongue. The demolished buildings for landmarks give you away. Your bed hasn't sat in Brownstone's hollow chest in years. There's no Yoruba present in your throat; no immigration letters in your back pocket. To come from is to lodge forgotten languages on twisted tongues. To miss the idea of several. To not [belong] anywhere that doesn't know how to leave. To come from is home when the place you learned to ride a bike isn't where you left it. When home no longer greets you like a friend home for a holiday but a stranger, overstepping boundaries. Invading territory. Appropriating. To come from doesn't mean to come back to, referring to the wanderlust that shape shift. you cannot remember leaving. To come from is to leave afro puffs bopping between two ropes on corner. Black woman weeping in worry, singin' in laughter, smile climbing from her throat dancing. To come from is to always use the word home, with a tentative definition.

When Blk Cracks

He says *Black* like it hurts,
like he's afraid to offend the white people,
call attention to his *Black.*
He say *Black*
like he know death in *Black* and he don't wanna catch it.
Like a whisper,
He paused before, to prepare himself.
When he say *Blackmen*
it be all rushed like stampede, he smushes the words together,
you see his eyes shift to each face quick.
The class don't notice,
but I do.
Same way I notice his head bow
when I talk about cultural appropriation
or the racism in the wind here,
                    the sports here,
                    the classes here.
There are only two of us here.
He hates it when I try to make things about race,
call attention to the way we sit different.
He don't want nobody to notice;
think we past it
calls himself evolved
                    modern
                    post racial
says "there's no need to talk about it."
But his skin say **Black,**
says hear me clearly
so **Black**
Common's name slipped off his tongue without his permission,
he couldn't help it says *Black.*
Before class he sponges his fade
and **Black** screams,

while his lips still whisper, halt and stumble.
We were the only two who knew Rodney King
& ain't that because of this **Black?**

They call me Black everyday.
My mouth says Black like its a part of Black,
like why would I want to be anyone other than **Black?**

I wonder when's the last time he had to own the (k)night in his skin.
Is that why he's so afraid to claim it?
He says *Black* like how dare I make him remember,
like he chose here for a reason.
He don't want this **Black.**
He just wants a break before he cracks.

Hit 'em with the Left

"We from Brooklyn my nigga,
Sometimes you gotta embrace the ratchet."
— L Ambitious

I like to pearl my Backwoods
there's pride when the leaf fucked up
& everyone else wanna quit
garnish that shit & start fresh with a new pack
& then there's niggas like us
who've never had the luxury of quit & tarnish
who like fixing impossible shit
find joy in the perfect pull
that can come from the rubble
– we come from the rubble
the chard brownstones imploding on themselves
still give us heat this is all we've ever known:
to make magic of the black and burning

the way the halo still sits pretty
even when its barbwire tented
we've tried to preserve people
that dissolve in a strong wind
watch smoke unwind brow & disappear
we choose ones oblivious to holes in their overcoat
that's how we used to be
rolled up - at the bottom of the pack
watching Brooklyn overflow with new white
forgetting about niggas like us
until the pull wasn't tight enough to cloud erasure
& Halsey street felt too safe to be our same home
& nobody felt like being displaced, moving again

y'all lined him up perfect
s
 t
  a
    g
    g
     e
       r
        e
         d

                    s   p   r   e   a   d
                    blendingnight'sshadows
the way they expect us to

he hit the floor after one mollywhop & we knew
from that & the quickness of sirens concerned
he wasn't of the rubble ready to defend
or think twice about coming out after dark
unprepared to fight for morning
the way we always have

I understood so I did what I do best,
pearled the loose ends, tucked tight
all the things we didn't want to come back to us
left him gutted on the corner because
if that ass get hit hard enough he'll go back
to his own fucking neighborhood and leave our hood shit alone

11

HandMeDowns

My family pass down truth like rites of passage,
like every family, there are years we act like never happened to maintain
a stained glass image of family, perfectly standing on a fracture.
We un-scroll darkness seldom & hostile.
I can't remember seeing

~~because I was young,~~
~~because I've always been absent~~
~~weekends were not enough.~~

most of what I have is pried from gummy mouths
whispered long after there's time to save anyone
from years we swallowed, buried and hid:
bodies stitched & smoked in blood, rotten teeth
and thinning hair. From bail money fashioned
from late night card games and prison visits
while the kids are at school. "Man #1" ignores.
Aunt #7 covers, We get up the next day
like stench doesn't linger.

No one told me the way the drugs laced their way into our bloodline.
In _____'s spliffed cigarettes, in uncle X's marriage, in the garage,
in my father's hands & their quickness to strike a woman's face,
their lack of softness when it swells,
No one taught me to tell when any of them were too drunk or too gone to
drive.
I don't remember how old I was when I learned to make _____'s drink,

I remember my cousins.
Owen wanted to be a tattoo artist and practiced on himself.
He was the prettiest of us.
I learned every Karina Paisen song just to sing with KayKay
in store run car rides, loud with the windows down.
It was they who showed me our family- after my bedtime,

the faces slashed and pit-bulls bought.
things that come back to bite with hands we watched grow.
Every family has their ways of sweeping and calling it love.

Owen's schizophrenic,
but XXX put the beer in his bottle,
*** ignored his blurring eyes, never gave him time to grow, nurture.
We a family with generations of fucking kids up & blaming them for their
regeneration
& I hide
in dreams & memories of my cousins telling me I was the smart one.
Of Owen at 23 telling me he can't read too good but he's glad that I always
do.

I have learned to find beauty in every mangled horror story
before the wreckage and every day after,
my family is both the riot and the communion,
the loudest laughs and the biggest army,
the lightning and the calmest winds.

The disease of hiding,
of keeping the family secrets,
of whispering selectively into pre-approved ears,
will not spread to me.

Momma's Afrika

My mother's emails start:
THIS IS WHY WE NEED TO MOVE!
She googles prices of land in Africa in her spare time.
Years ago, she stitched her Africa to her arm
ink seeped & made permanent. She's proof now
to ease the heavy of this month's mortgage payment.

Her adinkra symbol strips America's tint from her brown
puts a Nigerian glow beneath her eyes.
She remembers her promise land,
practices her accent in the mirror,
tastes the Yoruba, honey on her tongue.

She never holds English words this way.
Always violent. Angry. Snapping.
Her white people at work call her black woman
Momma says: They've modernized
a system designed to prey on melanin
This skin. This Black.
It gets worse here everyday.
Wouldn't you do anything to be free?

I can't tell momma my Africa don't look like hers no more.
My bones are set different,
they never learned to leave.

To make her smile I stencil
adinkra & Yoruba to my forearm
but it reeks of poetry, rebellion, America.
It makes a mural on my skin
& barriers between us.
Momma says they're taking my mind.
I've shortened my name.

I don't pray anymore.
History's coming for us.
She understands she can't protect me.
Often says, "I taught you what these deaths,
these laws, this war means
so why won't you leave with me?"

Nothing is permanent, her tattoo is fading.
I'm afraid she'll rot here waiting for me.

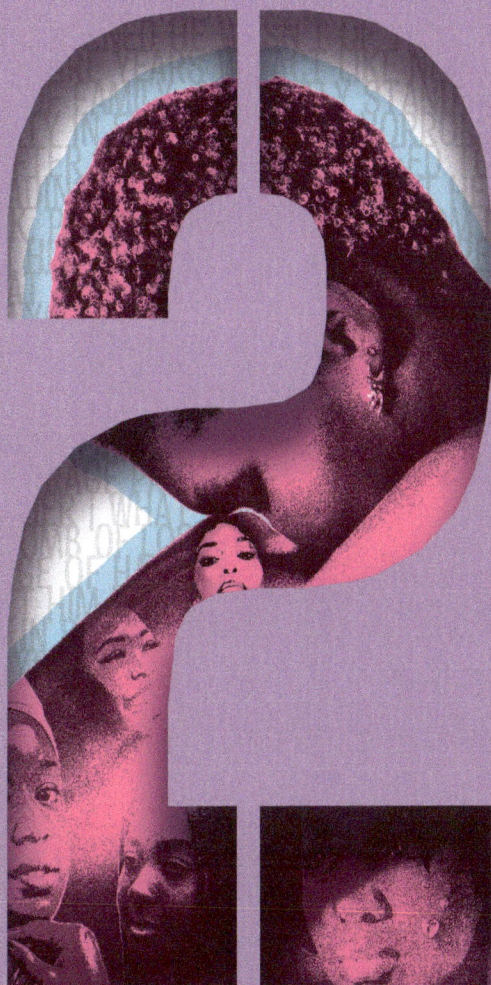

IF
I
HAD
A DIME
FOR
ALL
THE
WOMEN
I'VE
BEEN
BEFORE.

Fool

An Erasure of Lee Ann Womack's "The Fool"

I know

I don't

    see me.

hear my name

  be   introduced:

the fool

  still   love

a minute.   drink

something,

    crazy.   sleep

  call   you

    first,

  hard

    love.

a fragile thing,

      make

         my dream.

I go

  put

  him, and that

girl I've seen   around

    his heart, in   m y   hand.

  breaking mine,

'cause

who's still in love, with

love,   the fool.

Lessons from Lil Kim #1

When a man says he got you,
when he cleans the glass from your feet,
unbraids every knot in back,
pulls your skeleton from department store
and swells belly full;
It is okay
if he leaves sometimes.
It is okay to become stencil on wall,
tracing of wallflower,
echo.

It is okay if he never comes back for me.
It is okay if he comes back for you.

Jealous

An Erasure of Labrinth's Jealous

jealous   rain   falls   on   skin   close.   My hands
        been   jealous   of the wind   ripples
through your clothes,   closer than   shadow.   jealous
wind   wished you the best
    this world could give and   left   nothing
to forgive.   I   thought you'd   tell me   you found
    heartbreak and   it's hard.   I'm jealous
        happy without   the nights   I don't spend
        wondering who   next   I'm   the nights
jealous   love   gone   to share
        'cause   the best   world
    give   when   there's nothing   but

misery..   for me
    I sink   slip through   die
    another day,   behind this smile..
        when you left me
        I   thought you'd   tell me   you
found   a   heart   and

        Without me,
it's hard.

21

Live in this World

After Ntzoke Shange

I usedta live in a world the sun loved to abandon.
Gray.
Loud.
Silhouettes of budding brown girl bodies like mine
moving,
talking
close and   far,
at the same time.
Mouths
moving,
                  but nothing real being said.
I moved within
myself.
My world about five feet and two inches
of all the heavy. a woman in the world,
soft and broken at the exact same time ain't safe.

                                   ~~Retreat.~~

I stay alone.
When the sun says its daily goodbye,

                         everything turns ugly.

Don't do me no good
to meet a tall,
        short,
           black,
              ~~white~~
                young/old man,

who gets power from taking my things in the dark.
sun tries to take power from women like me and leave.
In my universe of five feet and two inches,
                I always have power.
I usedta live in your world,

really breathe in the world.
Free.
Sweet-talking.
Cloaked in honeystickykisses,
calloused from toe   to heel,
always
walking,
dancing,
moving.
Body,
a black,
        brown silhouette
with an ache from gyrating
always dancing,
throat always coated with vodka or whiskey,
ain't feel right if there wasn't a burn there.
                        I can't be that woman now.
covered in so many things,
                people,
who don't take care of my skin,
                my heart.
It's such a rip off.
Being in the world like everybody else.
Always talking but never really saying anything.
Always moving but never really going anywhere.
I usedta
be a black,
        brown,
                calloused,
                        dancing frame of woman in your world.
Known for losing control of my curves in the darkness,
I ain't neva had no rights to your world,
kept tryna swallow me whole when the sun turned her back.
                What a way to live.
23

The Best of Us

I remember the smell of collarbone,
bodies bunched on stiff bleachers.
The smell of grass on everything.
Lace of fingers.
Softness of eyes.
I remember running hand nose to lips.
Fighting covers. Cold feet.
You'd get mad. & I'd smile.
Laugh sometimes.

Remember the empty music room,
spoon fed Chinese,
cookies mushed on mouth.
I remember accent's slip from tongue
and slide down backarch.
Callused hands warmed frozen limbs.

I can still feel the breath of those days.
Everything was sweetheart good morning.
We wanted what we had,
ones who can't help comeback,
on small town back roads.
Headlights.
Shadows.
3am and stars watching
this body free of knot and kink.
Softer - comfortable that way.

Believe it or not I remember the air.
Pollen filled & timing perfect.
Learned to carry leaves, sunset colored and us.
Small things are first to go.
I can't remember the years,

that couldn't stay on this tongue.

But I remember that wooden gazebo.
You can't forget the hope in being that loved,
changes the way the spine sits, naturally.
This is coping
but we were happy once.

I don't need to remember when there was music.
Dance steps learned in brim filled garage parties.

So dark & roaring you could only see feet,
shade of hips, sag of jeans.
It's true, I'm selective.
I don't remember whose back broke first,
but I know at one point
there was the very best of us.

Lessons from Lil Kim #5

Mother tells me father is spill.
I have always been mop.

Because I am always here,
he'll never be less stain.

He's made my spine with "bend
just for this."

It is the him in you
that never really stops & leaves.

Mom, I have this recurring haunt,
this bone-strength-whatever-the-fuck

is the stench of father in this spine

There's a spill in my bed, mom
He reminds me so much of father

You'd hate him.

Pineapples

The first time, he said it was sexy.

Let his fingers cup my ass,
ignored my mustache stained boxers
thick and grey - which were supposed to be lace,
supposed to be soft like inside.

He didn't even ask whose they were.

It was the first time a boy hadn't
 - and that was the sexiest thing about him.
He licked his lips at the challenge of having to wonder
how this girl could gender-bend sexy and still get him hard.

He said it's crazy but it suits you.

He let me siphon the moan at the back of his throat.
Only when his roommate was asleep could I
pull his hair, revel in the twists his face makes.

You could tell it hurt and he could tell I loved it.

He hated when I slapped his ass.
It didn't matter how dark the room was.
He said it made him feel weird, gay.
I tried to tell him how sexist it is to not bend back & return the favor.

This man is blues bruises, knows love through hard mouth.

He leaves handprints everywhere he touches, tears
open, as I listen for sound of snapping bones/back.
He wants to see what it'll take to make me shudder & drown
He says it don't feel the same when I keep my snapback on,

27

work down the shape of him and round my mouth gentle.

He forgets his eyes still roll back and close, mouth hangs, whispers God.
When eyes open he tells me I have no chill.
I play too much coming in here like a nigga, tryna fuck him.
It's weird looking down and seeing me like that.

He can't do it, fuck someone who fucks him the way he fucks.

He feels taken from his own skin.
He can't get past how much I look like I'm not supposed to be here.
The image of what I'm supposed to look like bent over
don't compare to the ways I've learned to throw my legs behind my head,

- not like question but command, the way the boys do.

I tell him I ain't swallowing shit and the splatter better miss me.
He rolls his eyes cause I'm not the type to let him use face as target.
Who takes pleasure in the rough of giving & asks for nothing in return?
Because that woman is a good fuck?

I'm supposed to want him in the guts, supposed to lay open and be taken.

He is a real nigga. Sex ain't hetero if his hair hangs lower than mine.
He can't handle changing roles, says he's too straight for that,
rather I'm too gay for his kind of sex, I better find a woman to do that shit
too.
Last year touching his ass at all became a hard limit.

Last time he had this issue with fucking because my hair was short.

He tries to time out what weeks I'll have braids.
Most times he ends up pulling them out.
I spend mornings redoing them before class or hiding the bald spots.

He says he needs something to pull.

He don't understand, I like pulling hard too.

Scenes

After Giselle Buchanan

There are nights when a montage of the women in my life
keep my heart throbbing,
nights my phone is a hotline for stabilizing broken hearts.

Scene 1.
I am 9 and can't understand my mother crying.
Her room is different,
him & his things are missing.
She doesn't try to contain her sobs.
I can sense a love has died here.

Scene 2.
The women have gathered in the living room.
My mother is angry,
telling her friend she needs a man who respects her.
Her face is cloaked with scars from all the men who haven't.

Scene 3.
I am 12, my lab partner walks with
books covering her stomach
she is 14, dating a high school senior.
Today she's walking funny.
Today he is walking a different girl to class.

Scene 4.
I am 13 my friend Leo tells me
My Taelor has been waiting at her locker with puckered lips for a week.
My body becomes too heavy to hold up,
like my mother, I don't try to contain my sobs.

Scene 5.
My best friend and I are walking home,

she stares at the brownstone on the left.
The next day
I ask about the house she says, "I like to see how my innocence is doing
but I'm reminded, I left it with someone who doesn't care about those
things."

Scene 6.
I'm 14 dating a guy who is almost family,
on my cousin's bed he is anxious and rough.
I am uncomfortable and not ready.
When home, I try to forget his name.

Scene 7.
My older sister repositioned her chastity belt to cover her heart.
She's come to me twice for the key,
each time returning it worn.
She mumbles, "He has two kids, he lives with his mom."
Months later they're still together,
She's bragging about how she's whipping him into shape,
she laughs, I don't.
I'm too busy listening to her eyes
saying, "locks only work when you're on the outside."

Scene 8.
My sister tells me the dangers of giving away all your sacred parts,
warns me of people who have a thirst,
who feel like grain and taste like salt.
I know he has hurt her.
She gives me his old key, saying
"locks sometimes, only attract people who care about opening them."

Resentme

An Erasure of Beyonce's Resentment

I wish I could believe   I'll be all right,
but   everything   don't
          feel
Loving   easy
                              you
          because

I.   time
                              pretend
                    forgive.
      I'm   full

                    over   hurt.
          how   another   mean   thing
                    gave   me
                         you. and I   change
          as   trust,
A   lie

                    hard
      I

                              resent

                    feeling   no good
                    for you like
      i   could   n   t   be   you,

      loved   more,
more than

          sacrifice
                    32

                    because you i
you i   you i   you i

            she
been   for   years
                                    by   you?

            crying   stop.
can't   cry   stop.

You   wasn't
                            hurt.
        look   you done   now.
I
            look
and see
                    half of me,
that bitch
                                    ha!
and   you.

33

The Session

After Jeanann Verlee

You've never been silent for this long
You're wallowing in something
Why are you so unhappy?

unrequited

don't get poetic
admit your unhappy

I don't want to be happy

Why not?

It's a thin veil
that masks

What about love?

It's never wanted me back
We hid in each other
from each other
we're cowards who know how to undress
kiss each other with knives

don't use metaphor

We were in love
grew in like ivy
or spin-

we?

is there a difference?
me

shouldn't there be a difference?

some souls are tied
every his step a tug in my chest
love's the sanity of me
all the smoke in me

Do you think that's healthy?

I'm still here. I am still here.

Do you think he loves you the same?

should love be so fragile?

34

what about the air

tell me about the relationship

there are sheets soiled with every matter
wash
rinse
repeat
a graveyard we always come back to

so you're obsessed

he's the only one not impressed by me

so you're self-deprecating

no

codependent?

A body should share its weight

so we're back to metaphor

laugh loud, full of ghosts breath

I wish

but you're unhappy

I'm alive
my skin still sticks to the bone
isn't that enough?
he comes home eventually

when he didn't
when he doesn't
when he leaves?

don't remember

you remember everything

the door creaked slowly
all the heat following close behind
after that there is nothing

then tell me about a time you remember

what do you want me to say
he walked off with all my stuff
god gives the heaviest to the strongest

35

not feeling is the only way to survive

so we're doing this today

everyday
light was not my friend
food was not my friend
I felt like I'd betray my skin
I ruined happy for us
how could I love me when I'd made him leave
sleep. smoke. the quench of it all became my stuff

no metaphor

there was no relationship
no metaphor to hide in
there is nothing to feel hollowheavyempty about
logically
we were always playing house on hollow graves
we never would have made it

is that how you rationalize?

there is no out here doc
there is no avoiding stingbitecutcry
it happens in leave and in stay
it is life I'm learning
or how I love
fact is the house will burn
whether from his fire
or the one I keep warm when he goes
there's no way out
there's just surviving
my skin still sticks to the bone
nothing is perfect
to leave is to stand on ledge side
take leap of faith
not everybody got wings doc
some people swim
not that I know how to do that either

36

3

I USED TO RECOGNIZE MYSELF, FUNNY HOW REFLECTIONS CHANGE

Go Blind

An Erasure of Etta James' I'd Rather Go Blind

it was over
when I saw you.
deep down in my soul
I saw   that girl walking around

blind.
see
you   love   so
that I don't wanna.   you leave
just   to be free.
I   was   just
your kiss and your warm
reflection.   the glass   held to   lips   cry

blind, boy
see.

see   me.

39

Behind Every Man

Is a woman who's helped him become every breath.
From cradle to grave, in her rib spaces,

she sanded every emotion down with her teeth.
She has sat up editing his papers, speeches,

watching his film, listening to his new tracks.
I've been the nameless shadow. Dried hard

wet spot lay comfortable in. Someone else.
who bought the track spikes & the Trans-pass

& the gas & the food & everything he's smoked in 6 years.
I've been the child support check, ghost of father's past and present.

If I'm counting the things my shadow's done for men I've fucked,
I always seem to swell meta in love & carry twice my size.

If I kept tally of the drunk broad bodies my sister and I
have brought back from traffic & police & everything else,

& told you the way they boast about their nights flirting with earth's edge
and edit out our hands dragging them home, tucking them in.

Would anyone believe stories of women who were never there?
If my girls were honest in the conversation of earning,

we'd have at least four more degrees, right now.
We learned every criminal justice & business course

between our own due dates, for boys only known in dorm rooms.
We spent years feeding the air & each other myths to soothe.

For every woman who's danced with the secret in her existence,
swallowed the aftertaste of success earned in a phantom's low whisper.

For all the down ass chicks, the ones you don't see
who give the most & never ask for a seat or a throne.

Who satisfy their thirst from watching him taste.
Who have never been seen in the final making of:

the primed proper committed educated Black man,
who hasn't acknowledged the generations of women

who have bent & carried & stood somewhere out of camera angle.
Some men like to act like they came out good.

Like there weren't women who twisted themselves faint
every day to lend their shine. Their lives been a group project

done on time because of Black women's hands,
that are worn more than we've ever been praised.

Why We Let Them Stay

1
The women on my father's side all share their men.
It is something in this blood that only knows how to spread.
Let men come back. My aunts inherited from my nana, sympathy
for men in tough situations, mouths that always say come home.
Grandpa was in a tough situation. He was married
and nana always let him in.

2
Sleep comes for me different when I can't smell him
so I bend the lock every time. It's not about him.
It's that lonely looks so damn good 'til the walls start talking.

3
Air
body   sweats
break   outs
heat   churn
sorrow
riot

maybe this is what Nana felt.

4
Momma says it can't always be everyone
else but you, but what if Nana taught us gravity
is a work of God. Heart becomes a tomb of loss
and he always comes back. I admit that.

5
Love is a thin veil that lets me call this
something other than obsession. I'm always sorry,
when I'm not I'm at the feet of a man

who won't look me in the eye, working
to dismantle the bombs in me. This blood
is magnet for any man who can smell.

Afose

Most days I'm afraid I'll cut myself with my own tongue.
My mother tells me in Nigeria things are different.

There are systems in place
to avoid puncturing fragile things.
Maybe if I was home this could have been avoided.
There too, they've seen women split open
and still leaking from loss.
She says no one comes back the same,
some don't come back at all.
No one is supposed to go through this hurt
and be expected to go on like its normal.

It is a Yoruba custom to harness a gentle tongue.
Afose encourages meaningful utterances
Meaning if you say I hope he comes back,
understand that first means he will leave.

Which leads one to believe I created this,
I have tried to stop speak ~~anyone else~~
someone ~~else~~ better into this cavern and say ~~they'll stay~~
Each day is relearning.
Reprogramming the language to fit a world I dreamed
for so long, used this voice to bargain,
cement myself to a waiting I don't even want.

Sometimes I break my own heart just to feel something.
Let in even after logic and history and every god
have told me not to.
Just for the sensation of it.
Put a face to the song.
They say pluck it from the roots.
The one thing I remember from small fruit culture is about roots.

They're not easy to find whole.
If it's been years,
they can break into pieces,
each becoming its own family.

Unapologetic

I look unapologetic, like Black girl strong
with fresh timbs, tats and piercings.
Words seem bold leaving my mouth.
I walk my days unbothered.
Love myself. My skin. My hair. My body.
Let every hurt hate slide down my coconut oiled back,
got a clapback and knife for every situation.
Even my beauty is a resistance when my friends look at me
all they see is the way I still wake up every day,
praise me for my refusal to die, cry, crumble.

But I apologize.
I make myself smaller.
I'm afraid.   of dying.   being left.
of my heart bursting in my chest
because it's tired, aged heavy,
and still learning to name the love it wants.
It feels like I'm always in a state of wanting.
I'm afraid of not being wanted.
Every time someone laughs at me I break,
my body heats.

I edit
until I ache.
There's never a day that I don't want to change and
smear my black lipstick on thicker,
bolder.

My mouth quick to unhinge, shear and skin
but that don't mean I'm free.
I tone down,
sand down,
bite back,

depending on

if I love myself.
Sometimes living is the hardest thing there is.
I'm afraid if people knew everything
I've strong armed my way through,
they'll think I was doomed from the beginning,
they'll expect messy wind chimes to sound at every broken leaf.

I'm afraid of what'll happen when I can no longer pass.
Sometimes I love myself
& fit perfect for the unapologetic mannequin.
Sometimes I become just another Black girl,
whose anger is mask for things we're still not talking about.

For Girls With Moon Eyes & Brass Knuckles

Momma never told you there'd be days like this,
weeks like this,
years like this,
that will scratch your skin,
make your hair fall out,
turn your lips black,
everything black.
pull back every layer.

Distrust building
your spine, a curl of wind
you callous at goodbye.
I dare you to still be alive when it's over,
see magic in the mirror.
Find god in girl.
When men crawl from their burial plots
lusting for the smell of you,
don't stop waking up, getting out of bed,
hide it somewhere sacred,
tuck it in a crevasse.

Even when enemies are multiplying in your sanctuary,
everyday feels like a personal attack from god,
the voices begin to mix and none of them sound holy.
When every other word is goodbye, remember the way this skin never
leaves.
When the boy with soft eyes asks to play with your waist beads,
do not deny how rough his hands are.
When girls say they hate the way your words
force them to see themselves,
stop talking to them.
When all hands feel the same,
go back to talking.

When the bruises don't keep her from going back,
sleep with your phone on loud
be ready.

When your father goes to jail for the second time, feel nothing,
remember how hard your mother tried to hide the first.
When the boy in history class tries to pry good sex out of your half sleeping
frame,
get the knives,
get the hammer,
use the underwire of your bra like Auntie San taught you,
start locking your door.
be cautious.
not afraid.
Even when you can't remember what love looks like
and the boy you've unraveled for tells you
your time together are ghost stories he'll never tell his son.
Show him the dead things you carry
the ones he gives you
when he leaves and comes back
and leaves
and comes back
and leaves you waking up not knowing how you got here.

Momma don't want you to know about days like this.
Daddy still believes his little girl will never live days like this
but you survive days like this.

The scars morph beauty marks
and the horror stories tattoo themselves across the skin to say
I am still here.
I am alive
nothing can break me,
look how many have tried and failed.

49

Ibukun Kap*

So it is not come? Bleed me. Quiet. Bruised. Muse be
me, shakin' painted beauty; his verse oldlaced: white-
capped shy. Heaven agitate itself for mi
ornament, fam. Ya barrage of onyx palms tight

be da kinda beauty make beat brwn pride compare
cyan to seas God salt. & sure sun is a rich gem,
bore mourning, to all tucked things sacred like doves, rare:
Baton gutter Rouge, Fres(h)no sky clear- but them hems
make love stick, indent belief, my chakra aligned.
Word to Muva, Ghana, Ori bright I'm certain-

solid gold candles in the air of heaven assigned.
We're to break fast with praise, on time & amidst purpose.

Ibukun in Yoruba means Blessed, Kap in Sudanese means hood.

50

Bembe

I don't go to Bembes anymore.
Orisha come down like Holy Ghost
like Jesus come to crucify me
like one of the goats gonna eat my hurt
before we slaughter it.
The line of our white linen swaying
waiting to bend in praise
dobale for fate read like palm
for a fed tongue to tell us what salve we need
what ache needs the most attention
what destiny heaven imprinted on my back.
How can I stay in Orisha's good grace?

I shiver in this line
afraid to watch the shadow puppets beneath my bed dance
without permission
for everyone to start looking for the troubled darkness in my eyes
avoiding the uncertainty in right now while talking of a future I ain't sure
I'll see.

I had a reading in high school,
mommy took me.
The woman told us
I'd kill myself
if I really wanted to,
make sure I didn't really want to,
pulling out a secret I only shared with myself.
My mother's eyes widen and I shrank the whole way home.
She dug our hole and it moved into my chest.
I quieted
afraid of what next might be turned out for a cleansing.

My mother says from a Bembe home in New York:

Oya says stop it. & I'm caught
in headlights, analyzing
how I've lost my ability to balance
the priest in me and the Brooklyn born poet
who sometimes loves to fall,
just for the story.
I worry there's always someone to tell you you're going in the wrong direc-
tion.

& I think about all the times I've talked to the wind
begged Oya not to sweep me
leave me cringing small.
All the times I've prayed for a different heart,
one that don't stain as easy.
How many times have I avoided talking to my shrines?

Mommy says people hardly ever follow the instructions given in divination
and I know why,
because it's hardly ever what you need to hear.
All I wanted was a good day,
right then, where every step didn't drag
and someone to tell me the weight of my heart was okay,
normal even,
someone to tell me I could choose to stop drowning and wade.

Family Hands

My great grandmother's hands are soft from soil,
wrinkled from rocky mount from New York,
from two daughters and two grand-daughters and all four of us.
She goes to yoga that helps strengthen her joints.

Everything my nana's is swollen from so many things,
from Tuscaloosa markets in Black neighborhoods with the worst of meat,
from her Pepsi and pork bacon every day,
from being a well for everybody business.
The aspirin don't help all the gossip she hold,
she her own soap opera network,
her hands know everything & worked for it.

My uncle's hands are cemented in a curl,
been that way long as I can remember.
His beer cans and work wrench fit perfectly on the inside
Always, when he goes to hug, I can feel the calloused death
of them scratch my back before they warm me.

I don't remember my father's hands
but I have a feeling they're rough now too.
He has always held them stiff. In fists.
In the caress of drugs, he's been hard.

My momma hands are swollen from me.
I spread every part of her.
She told me to stop cracking my knuckles.

My hands are starting to get slower
harder to bend and snapback
Quick to wrinkle and develop a coat of ash
that seems to want to stay.
I use my hands for everything, always have,

crocheted sweaters and skirts
pried the carpets from hard wood
from Pepsi and pork bacon
from PA clay soil
from my lack of moisture regime
from familial obligation.

Safiya Washington is a writer, educator and performer from Brooklyn, New York, living in Philadelphia. She received her Bachelors in English Literature in 2016 and her MFA from Rutgers University in 2018. Safiya has been featured on CNN, and has toured varying colleges and universities. She is an international grand slam champion and is the recipient of a fellowship from The Watering Hole & Summer Literary Seminars (SLS).

www.ingramcontent.com/pod-product-compliance
Lightning Source LLC
Chambersburg PA
CBHW050015090426
42734CB00020B/3277